LACING UP

THE FIRST STEPS OF MY

RUNNING JOURNEY

IAN MORGAN

i

Table of Contents

Preface

Like life, this book is just one chapter of a work in progress.

The ideas that helped shape this collection of what I learned in my first years as a runner, started when I began sharing posts on Instagram about my weight loss/transformation journey.

And after replying to many of the comments, I found there were certain key points that my followers kept asking about.

Eventually, I put these points together in a list, and added a bit more detail. Mostly about what worked, and what didn't work for me. And from that list, the basis of this book was formed.

I cover what I experienced, and how it transformed me from a middle aged, overweight businessman, to a marathon runner.

So let´s kick things off with a brief introduction and a bit of background about myself.

My name is Ian Morgan, I was born and raised in a city called Christchurch, in the central South Island of New Zealand.

I'm a dad to 4 grown up kids, I was married, then divorced, single, (and then I got married again recently to my current Chilean/Spanish wife Fran, who is also a runner/ultra runner).

I worked in many different industries, from engineering (Auto industry), building and construction, property investment, trading in commercial equipment, various management roles, and a number of other jobs.

I lived in a normal 2 storey, 5 bedroom, suburban house. Had a couple of cars, and some pet cats.

I was reasonably responsible, earned a good income, and considered myself relatively level headed.

However things were about to change. There was something missing in my life, and the path I was on didn't fulfil me.

So how did I go from this life, to losing 30 plus kilograms and running marathons ?

This book will help to answer that question.

It's a collection of my personal experiences, the ups, the downs, and the eventual lessons I learned at the start of my running journey.

I discuss several key points that helped me make lasting changes to my physical and mental habits. These points have been the ones I've used to transform not only my body, but also to change how I think, and how I live my life each day.

Everything in the following chapters is written about what I've actually experienced myself, the things I learned, and how I applied what I learned.

I've included my top tips on what's worked for me, and the actions I took to make lasting positive change.

So let's get started.

Chapter 1
Endings and New Beginnings

There I was, another evening sitting on the couch after a long hard day at work.

The day in day out routine of deadlines, stress, and sleepless nights, was wearing me down.

The TV commercials flashing promises of happiness if I brought another new car, the latest computer, or the next generation smartphone.

I was an expert on this, as I had a house and garage full of 'stuff' that I had worked hard to accumulate over the years.

The constant stream of advertising messages telling me to 'buy more products and my life will be better, you will be a better person, and you will be happier'.

But the truth is I wasn't happy, I was overweight, unfit, unhealthy, stressed, and to be honest, I no longer believed that true happiness and fulfilment was found in purchasing and owning more stuff, or making more money.

As I sat there, drinking another beer to numb myself from feeling anything, so I could momentarily disconnect from this never ending cycle of work/ earn/ buy/ repeat. Something inside me changed.

I'm not sure why it happened this particular night.

Was it the emptiness I felt after years spent in the pursuit of becoming a good consumer?

Or maybe I was done with the need to be seen by my peers too 'do the right thing', make more money, pay more bills, and fit in with the middle aged, middle income demographic I now found myself trapped in.

As I sat there, my mind wandered back through

my life, to a time when I truly remembered feeling pure joy and happiness.

To those long summer days when I was a kid, days that I spent exploring the streets, hills and forests behind the house I was raised in.

That feeling of the sun on my face again, the smell of the pine leaves in the summer heat, and the simple joy found in the freedom of movement, as I ran between the trees, without the burdens of the world I had now created for myself.

Now before I get all nostalgic, I gotta point out I didn't have a magical easy childhood, it had its own challenges, however that's a story for another time.

That being said, I do recall many moments I enjoyed as a kid that stayed with me, especially a strong connection with movement and the outdoors, and it's something that I never really lost.

Then it happened, like being hit in the back of the head with a lightning bolt! An overwhelming feeling to experience running free through that forest again, the accumulated burdens and fears falling away, and a desire to fully embrace the feeling of being that carefree kid again, where the only thing I needed was the breath in my lungs, and my legs to carry me.

It's a bit to soon to cue the inspirational music just yet. I was in my mid 40s, about 30 kgs overweight, slightly drunk, and for a number of years, the biggest physical effort I made, was getting up off the couch to go get more food, or grab another beer from the fridge.

But this feeling was overwhelming, I just knew I had to get up and go run, right then, at that moment, no matter what!

I put down my beer, and walked out the back door, wearing jeans, casual shoes, and a cotton t shirt.

Ok, at this point, you may be thinking I was losing

8

my mind, and to be fair, I did actually consider it myself.

I didn't really understand exactly why I was doing it, but it just felt right, so I started to run.

I realise this sounds a bit cliche, almost like a scene taken from a Hollywood movie. However, unlike a movie, instead of soaring like a bird, I ran out of breath about 100 meters down the street.

My jeans were soaked in sweat and chaffing my inner thighs, it felt like every muscle in my body was on fire. And anyone driving past me in my neighbourhood at that time, must have thought I was running away from someone.

I certainly didn't look like a runner, hauling my 105 kg body clumsily down the road in casual clothes, puffing and sweating away.

But I was hooked, life had flicked a switch, and something deep down inside me had changed. Little did I know, that this moment would set me on a new course. One that would fundamentally change my life, and in the process, also change me in ways I never imagined.

Chapter 2
Breaking Bad Habits

I had started running, and it was such a relief to find an escape from the daily stresses in my life.

When I was out training, my thoughts became quieter, and I found a new kind of serenity in the simplicity of breathing in and out, and placing one foot in front of the other.

All the issues associated with work, the relationship problems from the breakdown of my marriage, and the general day to day noise of life, would start to fade away.

I could tune out and simply be present in the moment.

While all this was great for my mental health, I found that as I began to run more, there were some practical running related matters that required my immediate attention.

First on the list was my lack of suitable running apparel.

After looking in the back of my wardrobe, I found some old Asics sports sneakers I had been using for casual walking, some well worn basketball shorts, and a T-shirt with the word RUN appropriately printed on it.

Now I looked a bit more sporty, and in my mind, believed I was ready to take on this new challenge. It was time to develop a regular running routine!

And quite possibly, that's where this story could have ended.

Why's that you may ask?

Well, It quickly became apparent that the sneakers I was using, were not suitable for moving my 100 kg plus frame around, and my 'running clothes' were not moisture wicking or chafe free.

With blisters, sore ankles, sore shins, sore knees,

sore hips, and some fresh patches of raw skin in unmentionable places. I wasn't off to the best start.

And the thought had crossed my mind on a few occasions now, that maybe running wasn't for me.

However, a quick trip to the local running store was my saving grace, and I decided to splash out, and get properly fitted for some new shoes, and fully kitted out in some sweet new running threads.

After trying on several different outfits, I eventually walked out of the store in some brand new, shiny Mizuno runners, some short shorts, and an XL sized running T-shirt to help disguise some of my bulk.

Now I was ready to become a real runner...

But even though I had some dope new gear, and a ton of motivation to change, my body continued to protest. Which I guess was really no surprise after spending the last few years living such an unhealthy and sedentary lifestyle.

All the pains (including the chafing) soon returned, and I realised then, that even though the new shoes and clothing helped, this running thing was going to require a lot more effort, commitment, and some serious hard work.

This is where I began to learn the value of breaking bad habits, and how to replace them with newer, positive ones.

Mostly in life, when we try to break old unhealthy habits, we don't really think to replace it with a healthy new habit, so eventually we revert back to the habit we were trying to break (or replace it with an equally bad habit, like changing from smoking to overeating).

I learned this very quickly, and realised that to make any lasting change, I would need to find new habits that helped me work towards my goals.

So when running became my focus, I learned that

removing old habits that worked against me, such as overeating, drinking alcohol, and staying up late with the resulting lack of sleep. Would need to be replaced with new habits, like making healthy food choices, drinking water (or coffee), and setting up and following a good sleep schedule.

Doing this allowed me to break, and remove, the old habits, and focus my energy on the new ones I was building.

At first, breaking these habits and entrenched patterns of behaviour was hard, and I would be lying if I said changing them was easy.

But I guess it's a choice we're all faced with at some point. Change is either made by us, or forced upon us, and how we choose to adapt to it, is up to each of us depending on the skills and knowledge we have at the time.

Some of the ways I learned to develop better habits were simple, but also very effective.

For instance, I always struggled with getting up early, as I usually hit snooze on my alarm, and went back to sleep, and the thought of getting all my running clothes and gear ready when I was still half asleep, was at times daunting.

I would be banging around in the dark, trying to choose which clothes to wear, and waking up everyone in my household in the process.

I changed this by setting my alarm on my phone and placing it in the other room, so I had to quickly get out of bed to turn it off.

I also got my running gear out of my drawers the night before, and laid it out next to my phone.

That way when I went to turn off my alarm, my clothes, shoes, and gels etc were all there in one place, ready to go.

This became such a strong habit, that I still do it today, especially when I have a long run planned for the next day.

Once the new healthier habits started to take hold, I learned to accept them and eventually embrace them in my everyday life.

Chapter 3
The Daily Grind... (Finding Joy in the Process)

As my running settled into a regular daily routine, I figured out that setbacks were also going to be a recurring theme in my training.

My first major obstacles came in the form of overuse injuries from doing to much, to quickly. This resulted in me having to take time off running to recover.

At this point, the only type of exercise I did was running, I didn't swim, bike, or do any type of warm up, stretching, or strength/mobility training.

I was under the misconception that running a lot, would make me a faster, stronger, more resilient runner.

Looking back now, I realise I was basically breaking my body down, with way to little recovery time. So something eventually had to give.

Within that first year of running, I had a number of issues, starting with shin splints, torn calf muscles on both legs, sore knees, sore hips, sore lower back, plantar fasciitis, and a myriad of other aches and pains.

I'm sure I helped fund my local physiotherapists annual holidays within those initial 12 months, as I seemed to be in there every few weeks with one or more issues.

As a beginner runner, I was told by friends and other runners that injury was just a normal part of running, and over time I would get used to having time off training due to injury.

I struggled with accepting that this cycle of running and injury was to become my new 'normal'. There was no fun, or joy in my daily training, so I began to do my own research, and started to study everything I could find on the effects that running had on human physiology.

What I found, was there were many other things I should be doing as a runner, that would help to minimise the incidence of injury.

So I began combining these techniques with my regular running routine, to help me become a more resilient runner.

These other components were diet, strength and mobility training, recovery, and most importantly of all, rest.

Now I won't go into the details here, as I will cover these specific areas in a bit more detail in later chapters, but as I was to discover, combining these with my running allowed me to improve not just as a runner, but also with my general fitness.

My point here is that part of this first year of running (including my injury issues), taught me to start finding joy in the daily grind of training. I began to realise there was a lot of satifaction to be found in the process.

It allowed me to focus on what I want to achieve each day, keeping it in the moment, rather than looking ahead to see how far I have to go.

These small daily gains, combined with consistent action, started to yield positive results, as my running improved, and my injury issues became less.

It cannot be overstated how important it was back then, and how important it still is today.

Getting up and doing the workout I have in front of me for that day is all that matters. Being mindful of exactly where I am right now, and doing what I need to do, brings with it the simple satisfaction of achieving the task in front of me.

I must mention that I also started using online training plans during this time. And even though

I really had no idea what I was doing, it helped me to see the value in being more present, and enjoy each workout.

This was also the start of my process to eventually seek out professional coaching. But more on that in chapter 6.

Knowing how far, or how much 'time on feet' I had to run, meant I knew what I had to do that day.

So instead of looking at the weeks of training ahead, or stressing about my overall race distance, or difficulty, I only had to focus on what I had in my training plan today.

Breaking down months of work, or big race day goals, into smaller daily workouts makes what I'm doing much more enjoyable. I can keep my focus in the moment, and make the most of each training session.

Finding joy in the process is a bit like

compounding interest. By adding 1% each day, your sense of well being grows and multiplies over time. And after a year or two, this will add up to a solid investment return in your happiness bank .

Chapter 4
The Value of Consistency

To recap my first year in running, I would say it was a rollercoaster ride with some big ups, and a few downs, rather than some kind of steady progression, as I navigated my way through, not only the physical adaptations, but the mental adaptations as well.

Physically my body was changing, muscles that had long remained dormant, had been awakened. They had protested at first, almost like they were questioning what my mind was doing. But eventually that resistance changed into acceptance, and the tendons, ligaments, and other bodily systems, gave in to the fact that this 'running thing' was now part of my daily life.

It's amazing how quickly your body (and mind)

adapts to change once you begin to do something consistently.

I noticed during this time, how often my training, fitness, or strength, would reach a plateau. And just when it seemed like I wasn't getting anywhere, I would wake up one day, head out for a run, and find myself running faster and further with much less effort.

So often it would have been easy to think that I had reached my limit, and call it a day, however, just at the point of giving up, is usually where the next step forward (or magic) happens.

So often, I saw other runners I knew, giving up at this point. They had become stuck in a place where they no longer seemed to be making progress. So they backed off, believing they had reached their limit. After this, some gave up running completely, believing that there was really no point in continuing if there was no more room for improvement.

This is where the value of consistency kicks in.

Building your body and mind, day by day, week after week, over the course of years, will allow you to develop and grow. It's not the long runs, or the speed workouts, or the easy recovery jogs, it's doing all of these consistently, almost every day (obviously with some rest days thrown in as well).

So how do you become more consistent?

Firstly, focus on one goal at a time.

For example, when I was working on improving my running form. Instead of trying to change everything at once. I would pick one aspect, like foot-strike, and focus on that until it became a natural movement that I didn't have to think about. Then I would move on to the next goal.

Secondly, make slow and steady improvements.

Developing positive habits and making changes doesn't happen overnight. It may take weeks, months, or even years to permanently change old behaviours, turning up each day, and celebrating the small wins, will help keep you motivated.

Thirdly, don't let your emotions trick you.

Making changes through consistent effort can be a tiring process.

Your brain is always looking for the easiest way to get you through the day, sometimes it tells you things like 'you've done enough for today' or 'you can do it tomorrow'.

And while it seems like a good idea at the time, mostly its your emotions tricking you into taking the easiest path. Even when you feel tired and drained after a challenging day, you will be surprised how much energy you still have once you put on those running shoes and get out the door.

Lastly, accept that failure is part of the process.

We are all human, and we are all imperfect.

Maybe you miss a training session, or fall off the

healthy eating wagon, and go all out on a large pizza with a few beers.

Accept it, and get back on track the next day. The odd slip up is part of being human, keep moving forward towards your goals.

Consistency is one of the fundamental cornerstones of being a successful runner. Building a good base and maintaining it over time will allow you to go after just about any goal you set yourself.

It's like brushing your teeth every day, you gotta keep showing up and putting in the work to get results. There aren't any shortcuts on this one folks, you can't fake consistency, you can't wing it, you just gotta embrace it and make it part of your daily running practice.

Chapter 5
Developing Discipline

What is discipline?

The word itself originally comes from the Latin word discipulus (meaning pupil).

And I guess you could say I was becoming a 'pupil' of running. Studying and applying the information I learned, and seeing what the results were.

Trying out different training techniques on my own body, I found that this stage of my running journey was like taking part in a personal human experiment, testing out maximum weekly mileage and paces, nutrition, hydration, and pushing through my physical and mental boundaries.

I gotta point out that in those early months, many of my so called training experiments yielded less than satisfactory results. Especially some of the ones involving different nutrition options. Let's just say that there were some sudden and unexpected toilet breaks.

If I was asked how to explain what discipline means for me. Simply put, my definition would be 'doing what you gotta do regardless of what you feel like doing'.

Applying my definition of discipline to my own training played an important role in helping me form better fitness habits.

Getting up at 4am during the winter in the dark, driving to the trails, putting on a head torch, and training in wet, cold, freezing conditions, will lose its appeal pretty damm quick.

Trust me, motivation has a shelf life, and once it runs out, there's not much left to fall back on if you want to keep making progress.

That's where discipline comes in.

Discipline means doing the task in front of you regardless of how you feel, or what circumstances you face. Discipline doesn't accept excuses, it requires you to turn up and do the work.

While motivation wanes, discipline stays, and developing discipline requires self honesty, and doing stuff you don't always feel like doing.

The key to unlocking self discipline is practice, practice, practice. The more you do it, the better you become at it.

Now many of you will think this sounds a bit cliche, and this whole pushing through the tough times dialogue has been covered by others with a lot more experience than me. But really there isn't any secret to this, discipline is about carrying out tasks again and again no matter how you feel.

So what can you do today to help build self discipline?

Firstly, its about knowing yourself and knowing

which areas you struggle with.

Here's a simple exercise you can try.

Write down all the tasks you perform during a day, then look at the list and see which ones you procrastinate around doing. Make a list of the tasks you are putting off, and then add a new action plan around doing those tasks such as, ´I struggle to run in the morning, so my action plan for tomorrow is I will get up earlier, eat something that gives me energy, and get out for my run´

In this case, discipline will help you do the tasks you are trying to avoid.

Secondly, don't wait for it to feel right.

We all say things like, ´when I have enough time / money / energy, then I will get it done´.

Well, the moment to do what you gotta do to work towards your goals is right now. You will never be 100% ready, so get started and do what you can today.

Thirdly, follow a plan and track your progress.

Having a training plan, and checking in each week to see how you're improving, will give you a mental boost, and give you feedback, that what you're doing is helping you move closer towards achieving your goals.

Lastly, remember that developing discipline isn't about creating perfection, its about practice.

You're gonna make mistakes, and things you try won't always work out.

It's ok, developing discipline is basically the act of trying , failing, figuring out why it didn't work, and trying another way.

In a nutshell it comes back to the heading of this chapter, 'developing discipline' which is about being a pupil and always being open to learning or 'developing' as a person.

Discipline isn't a destination that you arrive at, its a lifelong process that is about knowing yourself and your weaknesses, and learning to manage them through the creation of better physical and mental habits.

Chapter 6
Time for A Coach

After about a year of running, I was making some progress, and I reckoned it was about time to dip my toe into the racing scene.

At this point I had no idea what racing would be like. I was nervous and excited, and I couldn't wait to apply what I had learned so far.

However I also understood that my approach to training was still a bit hit and miss, and while I was learning (mostly from my mistakes), I realised if I was going to progress, that some coaching would be a good idea.

So after asking around a bit, I decided to join a local running club.

This was one of the turning points, and a big step in my progression from an amateur hobby jogger, to a more focused runner.

Being part of a group of runners, where I could tap into a vast array of knowledge about all aspects of running, was extremely valuable.

I was keen to find out as much as possible, and after a few sessions I had figured out there was a big gap in what I thought I knew, and how much I still had to learn.

These early coaching and group run sessions helped me to understand that running wasn't just about the physical aspects, but also how nutrition played an important role, and that the mental challenge was one of the most important pieces of the puzzle to master for most runners.

And purely from a social perspective, It was great to be part of a supportive group of people, who shared a similar passion for running.

There were also some great coaches in this run group, and I listened intently to their advice, and their own experiences.

Of course the reason I wanted coaching in the first place, was to get ready for racing, and so began my first targeted training program to run a half marathon.

I´m one of those runners that thrives on the structure of planned training, and I quickly found that this is what was missing from my training prior to being coached.

I loved the weekly progression of following a plan, the gradual building of distance, the edition of more intense track and interval sessions, and the weekend long run.

These all helped me realise what I was missing in my training before.

After being in the running group for a while, I also started some one on one coaching to work on things like my running form, strength training, and ocasionally joining in with some of my coaches training sessions.

I found that as I improved, I required more targeted training sessions (like speed work or tempo runs), that involved me running alone.

It was during this time, my coach had a chat with me, and said that he had pretty much taught me everything that he could.

So he suggested looking for a new coach that would help me grow further in the direction I wanted to go.

I'm grateful he recognised the fact that I was ready to move forward, and that shows a level of maturity and respect, knowing that I now needed someone else who could continue to help me grow, and become a better runner.

I asked around and found a new coach with the experience I required to move forward.

Since then, I've used a couple of other coaches, and each one has been invaluable in helping me get the best out of myself.

So how can having a coach help?

Firstly, a coach can provide motivation and support.

A coach will usually be the voice of reason, which will help you prevent over reaching in your training and racing. They will know when to push hard, and when to rest and recover.

This will help you lower the risk of injury, and maximise your chances of turning up on race day ready to go!

Secondly, they can improve your performance.

Coaches design personalised training plans to systemically build performance to help you achieve your running and racing goals. This can also include other aspects of training, like advising you on strength training, recovery, and sometimes nutrition.

Thirdly, they teach you the correct way to train to

suit your lifestyle.

Helping you to avoid common running mistakes like running too much, too soon, or not taking any days off to rest and recover.

They will help you to maximise volume and intensity within your weekly schedule, and help you avoid overtraining and burnout.

Even things like checking your running form and making suggestions to help correct any issues that may lead to injury.

And lastly, a coach can help guide you in the process of reaching your running goals.

This is a biggy! Finding a coach you trust, and believe in is so important. Having someone there to support and guide you through the highs and lows, will make training so much more enjoyable for you.

A coach helped me to learn to immerse myself in the day to day grind, and trust in the process, teaching me the value of patience, and once again, reinforcing the value of consistency and hard work.

I can't emphasise enough how important joining a run group, and using a coach was for me. The value they add, and the physical gains I made using a personalised, well structured, flexible training program, allowed me to grow, and improve my fitness to help me achieve my running goals.

Chapter 7
Mindset, The Mental Game

There's a fine line between passion and addiction, and I guess what constitutes borderline obsessive behaviour, is subjective depending on your individual point of view.

I reckon there are certainly times in my running journey you could use the words 'borderline obsessive' to describe my love of running and racing.

And from a purely analytical perspective, I would probably find it hard to disagree with you.

This brings me on to mindset.

Specifically, how the way that you think, and what you believe, will have an impact on what kind of reality you create for yourself.

The following explanation is an example of the power of mindset. This is one I learned from personal experience when I was trying to achieve a specific time goal in a race.

Let me explain.

One of my goals was to run a sub 3 marathon, and on paper I had the training to back it up. However whenever I got close to my time goal during an actual race, I just seemed to miss the target.

So I made a race day strategy, and went through it again and again in my head, and then visually imagined myself running each part of the course, and crossing the finish line with the time on the clock I wanted. I replayed this many times over in my head, until mentally, I convinced myself I had actually run the race and finished in this time.

Come race day, It felt like everything was in place, and I just set my mind on auto pilot, and let it follow the script I had already rehearsed in my head many times over.

And guess what? almost exactly what I had visualised in my mind, played out in real time on the race course, and I crossed the finish line within seconds of my planned time goal.

Now the more interesting part of this, is once I had mentally and physically broken this time goal, each time I've ran the marathon distance since, I've ran it faster and consistently beat my initial sub 3 hour limit, a barrier that I previously struggled to break.

You could argue I'm now fitter, or a better runner, which could explain the faster times.

But my training since hasn't focused so much on road races, and I've actually run the last 2 marathons under more challenging circumstances.

I reckon it's because my mind now believes I can do it, and it has the real world experience to back that up. Mentally, the barrier that was once there has been removed, and has now been replaced by a new reality.

The body follows where the mind tells it to go, and I can certainly say there's some truth in that.

Now I gotta add in a disclaimer here.

I'm not saying that just believing something is actually enough to make it happen or guarantee you will achieve it.

However when you truly believe it, do the the work, form a plan, and execute that plan, your chance of success goes way up.

Here are some of my top tips I use to help build a positive mindset.

Firstly, talk positively to yourself.

It's estimated you say 300-1000 words to yourself per minute. These words are similar to your diet, in the sense that what you put in, is gonna determine the end result.

So make sure you feed your mind (and body) with the right stuff.

For example, when something doesn't work out as expected, rather than saying 'this always happens to me' or 'things never work out', instead try, 'this happens sometimes, but it's not a big deal'.

You see how the first phrases from the conversation you're having in your head, come from a place of permanent negativity or pessimism, whereas in the last phrase, you're coming from a place that whatever went wrong was just a temporary situation, and the conversation in your head is more optimistic.

Secondly, practice visualisation.

Many times before a race, I've visited both the start and finish line.

When I'm at the start line, I imagine feeling well rested, calm, and strong.

And at the finish line, I visualise myself running those last few hundred meters, feeling elated, and raising my arms and smiling as I cross it.

I also visualise the race, and cover all scenarios, like what will I do if the weather changes, or if my nutrition plan doesn't work as expected. Visualising possible issues before they happen, and imagining what I will do to manage them is a very powerful tool, and allows me to keep a clearer head, and change my strategy when things don't go to plan.

Thirdly, use simulation.

Now you have the image in your mind, use it and go simulate how you plan to race.

For example, If I'm training for an event that is in the desert, I may not have access to that kind of terrain. However, I try to find a beach or sandy area nearby, put on my desert running gear, and go run up and down sand dunes for a few hours.

This way I'm simulating the experience of running on soft sand, and carrying all the gear I will actually use in the race.

The same goes for night running, or running in the mountains. I find and environment with similar conditions, and train there.

Training as often as you can in a similar environment to race day will lift your mental (and physical) game.

Finally, believe in yourself.

Positive self talk, backed up by visualisation, and taking action with simulating what you're about to take on, will give you the tools to make your mental game much stronger.

In summary, using these various techniques backed with physical action, to train your brain to embrace a new reality, will set the stage to build new neural pathways that will allow you to achieve so much more.

Remember you create the reality of the outside world, by what you create inside with your thoughts, feelings, and beliefs.

A strong mental game is where most of the work happens, so train your brain just like you would your physical body, use visualisations, positive conformations, and then practically apply them to your everyday training.

Chapter 8
Food as Fuel, What I've Learned About Eating

One question I get asked a lot, is what type of diet do I follow. Let's just say if I got a dollar for each time someone asked me, I would be writing this book from my super yacht!

I gotta point out, I'm not a dietician, nutritionist, doctor, or scientist, I have absolutely no expertise in the areas of nutrition, or the biological effects, health benefits (or drawbacks) of the many different diets or ways of eating.

It took me between 6-12 months to lose most of the extra 30kgs I was carrying around. I also worked on building more muscle during this time.

Now some people will do it faster, some slower. There's no point comparing yourself to others.

Work with your body and your timeframes.

What I have learned is that our bodies are remarkably complex, and respond to how we eat in many different ways, at different times in our lives. There really doesn't seem to be a one size fits all approach when it comes to food.

However, in saying that, there is one general rule that just about every expert agrees on, and that is if you're in a calorie deficit, you usually lose weight. And if you're in a calorie surplus, you usually gain weight. Now whether you lose or gain fat, muscle, or water, will really depend on many things, including the amounts of protein, carbs, and fat you eat. But I just wanted to point out that with all the different types of diets, ultimately, it just seems to come down to an energy deficit/surplus equation.

So to share what worked for me, let's break it down into steps:

Firstly, the biggest change I made was to stop

eating highly processed foods.

Basically anything that wasn't grown or raised, so no more alcoholic drinks, donuts, takeaway pizza, burgers, french fries, sodas, potato chips, sweets etc.

If the ingredients list contained multiple additives, colours, flavours, and preservatives, then it was gone!

Now I know some folks say a little now and again won't cause you any harm. And yes, I agree with that. However, I also know myself well enough, and realised that what I needed at that time was a complete diet reset, where I removed the option to have 'just a little'.

I gotta point out that this was at the beginning of my dietary changes.

These days I have built up enough good eating habits, that I can now eat a cookie, ice cream, or have some chocolate, and not go back to my old unhealthy food behaviours.

Secondly, I started to look at what dietary changes I needed to make to help fuel my training and recovery.

This involved increasing my protein intake, eating healthier fats that were less processed, and eating higher nutritional value carbs in the times when my body used them the most (like before big races, and during training).

My diet before was high in sugary carbs and saturated processed fats (basically processed junk food), and low in quality protein (like chicken, fish, meat, and eggs).

I turned this around, and increased my protein intake (to help build more muscle, and assist in muscle recovery), while decreasing the amount of simple highly processed carbs.

Now I want to be clear, It wasn't a Keto diet, a carnivore diet, a paleo diet, or any other trending diet.

I just experimented a lot, and found what worked for me at the time.

Yes I still eat simple sugary carbs when I want quick energy. And I also eat carbs throughout the day too.

The way I used to eat, and the way I eat today is more about using a mix of protein, fat, and carbs during the times my body requires them.

Thirdly, I got some food scales and started to measure my portion sizes, and count calories and check things like my protein intake.

Yes I know, it's something most folks don't really want to do. But I did it at first out of necessity to actually track and measure what I was eating.

Currently it's not necessary, as I've got a pretty reasonable idea about how much I gotta eat based on my training load.

And to be honest, I enjoy eating, and don't want to

make my life all about counting calories and measuring portion sizes.

Lastly, I kept track of my weight over a longer period of time, because over the short term, I found weight loss and weight management isn't a liner process, and there are fluctuations.

For example body water levels do change daily, especially if you're training in the heat, and how well you hydrate before, during, and after training can affect weight by up to a few kgs post and pre run.

Sometimes you will hit a weight plateau. And you think you're not losing fat. The scales hardly seem to move over a period of time. However, it doesn't necessarily mean you've stopped losing fat. Muscles grow and get stronger and bigger with training, so maybe you're gaining muscle, while at the same time, also losing fat.

Remember that taking the average over a period of time, is better than basing your success (or perceived failure) over what the scales show you every day.

A longer term view, and looking for slow, sustainable weight loss and muscle growth, while maintaining energy levels, helped me to stay focused on the process to get done what I had to do each day.

Now there's nothing right or wrong with any type of diet, it's about finding what works for you, at your stage in life, and for what you're trying to achieve.

Running longer and longer, while building speed, meant I was looking to get stronger and more resilient to injury. So I wanted to build muscle and strength, and be lean enough to carry my own weight over longer distances.

That led to me increasing my protein intake, and changing my portion sizes to suit my training.

The flow on effect was losing fat, and gaining

muscle mass.

So most people want to know what an average eating day looked like for me when I started to drop my weight. And remember this is what I ate, and at the time it worked for me over a period of months. I will point out that this was a temporary measure to reduce calories to help me lose excess fat, and not a long term sustainable eating plan.

It is not dietary advice, and you should consult a dietitian or suitable nutritionist for personal guidance.

Breakfast:

1 large glass of water… (0 calories)

2 coffee's with milk (no sugar/ sweetener)…(60 calories)

2 pieces of whole grain toast with 2 teaspoons of sugar free/salt free peanut butter… (340 calories).

Morning snack:

1 coffee with milk (no sugar/sweetener)...(30 calories)

1 Apple... (90 calories)

Lunch:

200 grams chicken breast no skin ...(220 calories)

150 grams broccoli... (52 calories)

100 grams sweet potato... (94 calories)

2 glasses of water... (0 calories)

1 coffee with milk (no sugar/ sweetener)... (30 calories)

1 piece of 70% dark chocolate 8-10 grams... (45 calories)

Afternoon snack:

1 Apple... (90 calories)

1 coffee with milk (no sugar/sweetener)... (30 calories)

2 glases of water... (0 calories)

Dinner:

200 grams fillet steak...(520 calories)

Salad with lettuce, 3-4 tomatoes, half a cucumber, approx 1/2 a small avocado...(138 calories)

1-2 glasses of water... (0 calories)

1 Cup of black tea... (1 calorie)

Total calories per day = 1732

Total maintenance calories per day= 2400 (average based on 46 year old male with moderate activity levels)

Calorie deficit= 668

For the sake of simplicity, I didn´t include the nutrition I would eat on longer training runs. Generally, If they're longer than 80-90 minutes, I usually eat between 200 to 400 calories an hour. So remember to factor that in if you are working on creating a calorie deficit.

Here are the top nutrition tips I used during my early running years.

Firstly, get enough quality protein.

Depending on bodyweight and muscle mass requirements, make sure you actually get enough daily protein (if possible aim for approx 30-40% of your daily calories form protein).

Secondly, eat when you're hungry.

It sounds pretty simple, but if you're really hungry, your body is telling you something. If you feel full, your body is also telling you something.

And while I'm on the topic of protein, eating enough good quality protein will help your feel more satiated (full) for longer.

Thirdly, manage portion sizes, and plan meals ahead.

You don't need to fill up your plate just because it's big. Calculate nutrient requirements and plan your portion sizes.

To help with this, plan out your meal prep for the week, and shop accordingly. That way, you will know that you're getting the right amount of nutrients per meal.

And lastly, stick with it.

Yes, you will probably fall off the wagon occasionally, and binge eat pizzas, fries, and have a few beers. That's called being a normal human.

Start following your healthy eating plan again the next day, and put it behind you. I remember doing this numerous times at the beginning, and eventually, I became disciplined and consistent enough to not let it get in the way of working towards my longer term nutrition goals.

So in summary, as you can see from my average eating day when I first started to work on losing excess weight, there are no real secrets.

I worked on staying in a calorie deficit for a specific period of time until I achieved my goals.

I ate mostly healthy, whole, unprocessed foods.

And I focused on gradual improvements over the long term.

Chapter 9
Sorting Out My Running Form and Strength Training

Changing my running form was a game changer. Especially in reducing the number of injuries I used to have when I first started running.

Improving my foot-strike, cadence, and working on my strength and mobility training, all helped drastically reduce the incidence of lower leg, hip, and back issues I was struggling with in the first year or two.

What constitutes good running form is a little different for everyone, and there are not many of us who are naturally talented in this area. However it is something that we can learn, adjust and improve, to help make running more efficient, and to help reduce the muscular skeletal stresses we place on our bodies.

I'm not by any means an elite runner like Kipchoge or Killian, and there's enough information available in other books, or online, about the most efficient angles, pronation, and hip extension etc.

I'm just gonna go through what I learned, and how I applied it to change from an extended leg heel striker, to a mid foot, centre of gravity striker.

The first time I actually knew there were major issues with my form (apart from all the injuries), was when I attended a seminar on running form on a Sunday afternoon during wintertime, about 1 year after getting up off the couch.

I thought my form was pretty smooth up to that point, until I had my running gait analysis assessed on video, I saw the clip of me running, and realised I looked anything but smooth.

The good news is that when you become aware of a problem, you can then take the necessary steps to work on fixing it.

I spent the rest of that cold Sunday afternoon learning drills and techniques to improve my foot-strike, cadence, running posture, and even how to correct my arm swing (yes, I learned arm swing makes a difference, especially the further you run).

Here are some of the main points I took away:

Cadence counts (or count your cadence):

Cadence is the number of steps you take per minute when running.

The average suggested cadence is around 180 steps per minute. However that can depend on a number of factors, such as how long (or short) your legs are, your height and weight, and any bio mechanical issues you may have.

To help improve cadence work on decreasing stride length (basically take smaller steps).

In doing so, you will find your foot will more readily land under your centre of gravity.

One of my first coaches had a great way of showing the practical application of changing cadence and foot-strike. He suggested getting a metronome (or use a metronome app), set it to 180 beats per minute, and then skip on the spot without a rope. Once you get the rhythm right, lean forward slightly, until you feel you're almost falling forward, then start to run. The point of this exercise is to get used to your feet moving with a higher cadence, and to land under your centre of gravity. It's almost impossible to skip easily on your heels (try it). Doing this form drill will also help you develop a more midfoot/forefoot landing.

Foot-strike and knee-drive:

As mentioned previously in the last point on cadence, foot strike also plays an important role in reducing injury, becoming more efficient, and improving pace.

I found changing from a full on heel striker, to a

midfoot/forefoot striker helped me reduce the braking effect, let me open up my stride, and develop a more propulsive driving force in my gait cycle.

Learning to land mid-foot took me a few months to master, and I spent many hours of training, taking smaller strides, always thinking about placing my foot under my midline (or centre of gravity).

After a while it started to feel more natural, and I no longer had to consciously think about foot placement any more.

The second part of this equation that helped, was practicing knee drive drills. Helping to propel my body forward, and give purpose of direction to my stride.

Combining good foot strike and knee drive techniques helped me to increase pace and efficiency, while reducing overall running effort.

Breathing:

Here's one that I never really considered would make much of a difference, until I started to practice better breathing techniques.

Basically timing my breathing with foot strike (2 breaths in, one breath out), with a 1-2-3 rhythm.

Breathing is similar to how an engine works in a car, the more available oxygen we can take in, and the more carbon dioxide we can expel with each breath, the more fuel we can burn, and the powerful the engine will become.

Now that's an oversimplification of a more complex process, however there's a reason that athletes with a higher VO2 max perform so well.

Basically VO2 max is a mesure of how well your heart pushes oxygenated blood to your muscles, and how efficiently your muscles can extract that oxygen from your circulating blood.

As you breathe in oxygen, it powers a metabolic

reaction within your muscle cells, that gives your muscles energy called adenosine triphosphate (ATP).

You breathe faster and deeper while exercising because your body needs more oxygen to help it use the bodies available energy.

Developing good breathing techniques is often one of the overlooked parts of running form training, however it's another important piece of the puzzle to help improve efficiency, and become a better runner.

Arm swing:

Arm swing techniques will differ between road endurance running (like a marathon for example) and a trail event (like a 50km hilly ultra).

The techniques applied will be different for both.

In regards to road running, I remember my form coach telling me to imagine I had a cross drawn on my torso. Firstly a vertical centre line down the middle from my chin to my waist, and secondly a horizontal line about chest height. With each arm swing, I wasn't allowed to cross my hands over the centre line, or drive them above my chest line. Also I wasn't allowed to drop my arms too much below my hip height.

This gave me a small quadrant to work in, and helped reign in any excess arm movement that would use extra energy.

Also consciously thinking of arm swing, arm drive, and direction, helped when pushing the pace. Especially during those final finish line sprints.

Trails are a bit of a different beast, as arm swing changes depending on whether you're climbing or descending.

In the case of climbing, a less pronounced version of the road running arm swing will usually suffice depending on terrain. However on the downhills, a more open stance with arms out to the side (kind of like a bird spreading its wings) will allow you to adjust your balance, and help with sharp turns etc.

Strength training:

This is a very individual, and it really depends on many different factors, like where you're starting from, and what areas of your body need improvement with overall mobility and strength .

I believe the best thing for most people, is to go get an assessment from a professional strength and conditioning trainer, and discuss with them your training, racing and overall fitness goals.

You don't necessarily need fancy gym equipment, or expensive fitness memberships to get stronger.

Yes, gyms are a great place to get professional guidance, help you to stay motivated, form good training habits, and help you get stronger.

However in the beginning, for me, it was easier to

get a basic strength and mobility assessment done, and use an at home training program that would fit with my schedule.

I did purchase a basic home weights kit including a couple of kettlebells, some dumb bells with weights, a bar, a Swiss ball, a bosu ball, some exercise bands, and a yoga mat

(If you don't have access to weights or a gym, there are many simple bodyweight exercises you can start with that will work too).

I started working on my strength program in two areas. Lower body strength and mobility, and upper body and core strengthening.

Lower body training involved squats, single leg squats, reverse and forward lunges, box step ups (all the above can also be done with weights), and various Swiss ball and bosu ball ankle mobility, strength, and balance exercises.

Upper body and core training involved push and

pull muscle exercises, including bicep curls, overhead lifts, Russian twists (with variations) push ups (with various arm positions), various dynamic planks, window wipers, dead bug, and single/double leg raises on the yoga mat.

When I had access to a gym, I also used different weight machines, usually in a circuit with a set number of reps.

My training at this time consisted of first building strength, usually gradual overloading adaptive type training, like lower reps with heavier weights, followed by higher reps with lower weights.

Once I had built strength in the required area, my strength training became more maintenance based, adding in more specific workouts targeting certain areas, depending on what type of event I was training for.

For example, if I had a race with more hills, I would focus on building better leg strength to handle the extra load of the climbs and descents.

As I mentioned before, If you don't have weights, a simple 20 to 30 minute bodyweight circuit 3-4 times a week can be effective.

For example:

100 push-ups: 5 sets x 20 reps.

100 widow wipers: 10 sets x 10 reps.

100 double leg raises: 10 sets x10 reps.

50 Russian twists: 5 sets x 10-12 reps.

50 squats: 5 sets x 10-12 reps

50 reverse lunges: 5 sets x 10 reps (each leg)

Carry out 1 set at a time, with a 10-20 second rest between sets, and repeat until complete

 (do the maths to divide up the sets/reps in a suitable order)

You can also use furniture like chairs to change the

angle of push-ups etc. And add different variations on these exercises, depending on what areas you want to target.

Strength training is one area that's very important, not just for running, but in helping maintain an active lifestyle, especially as we get older.

We all start losing muscle mass as we age, and the old saying of use it or lose it definitely applies here.

Remember running form and strength training is such an individual thing, and form drills, or strength training that works for me, may cause possible injuries or create other issues for you or someone else.

So with that in mind, here are the running form and strength training tips that helped me.

Frstly, Relax: including your arms, shoulders, and your breathing.

We've all done it, hunched shoulders, clenched fists, and shallow heavy breathing. This will not only promote poor form, but will also make you feel fatigued much quicker.

Find a comfortable rhythm with your breathing and foot strike, drop the tension from your shoulders, and relax your hands. A chill runner is a happy runner.

Secondly, practice increasing your cadence.

Increasing cadence will help you to adjust different aspects of your running form more easily. With a shorter stride length, you will find your foot will start to land under your centre of gravity, helping you develop a more effective foot-srtike, and lead to a more efficient mid foot/forefoot landing.

Thirdly, Regular strength training.

You're better to do 4 x 30 min home strength training sessions a week, than one trip to the gym for a 2-3 hour full body session.

Break your training up into smaller chunks, and

you're more likely to get the work done.

Lastly, results take time, maybe months or years, Abs in 14 days is not an attainable result for most.

Be patient, it took me many years to get out of shape, and it took quiet a few to get back in shape again.

There really is no shortcut, or secret here. Just hard work.

There are many good personal trainers, fitness apps, videos on YouTube, Instagram, and TikTok in regards to running form and strength training techniques, and the drills associated with them.

There really is a wealth of information available, the only thing you need to do is make a decision to start.

In summary, running form and strength training is something I am always working on and learning about.

Making it a regular part of my weekly training has

helped make me a much more resilient and injury resistant runner.

Chapter 10
Set, Plan, Execute:
Putting Together What I've Learned To Achieve My Running Goals

I want to share with you the story of how I achieved one of my first running goals.

As you've seen throughout this book, in each chapter I've shared the things I've learned that helped shape the runner (and person) I've become.

The process is a bit like one of those kids picture books, where you connect the dots in a certain order, to create the overall picture.

When you start, you're just joining points on a page, however as you connect more 'dots' the bigger picture is revealed.

My earliest big running goal, was to qualify for, and run, the Boston marathon.

It's the worlds oldest annual marathon, and one that you have to run a qualifying time for to enter.

For my age group at the time (45-50), that meant running under 3 hours and 25 minutes, which looking back now, doesn't seem to hard. However, at the time I didn't have a lot of experience (or speed), and I was still relatively new to running.

So, how did I apply what I've learned to set, plan, and execute this goal?

By using the tips and stratagies, that I covered in the previous chapters, and joining all the dots together one by one.

I had to develop good training habits, that includes sticking to a training plan, eating well, and getting enough rest. As mentioned in chapter 2, breaking old bad habits, and replacing them with new healthy ones, allowed me to gradually build a stronger body and mind that could handle the marathon distance.

Once these habits became a part of my regular routine, I immersed myself in the day to day process of getting the work done. As you saw in chapter 3, finding joy in the process, not the end goal, will make the everyday grind much more enjoyable.

When you find joy in the process, you also find it easier to develop consistency with training, eating, sleeping, and doing what you gotta do to improve. The lesson of being consistent from chapter 4, was, and still is, one of the most important things I learned. Consistency in training over the long term helped get me to the start line of Boston.

Consistency and discipline go hand in hand. Chapter 5 mentions how important discipline is, especially when you don't feel like training, or life gets in the way. Discipline isn't about passion, or motivation, it's about getting up and getting the work done, even when you're tired, it's dark and cold, you've had a challenging day or night, and you don't feel like lacing up and getting out there to train.

Discipline will help prevent you falling back into old patterns of behaviour. Discipline kicks in when that voice in your head tells you to take it easy, and there's really no need to continue the workout or training run. Discipline gets you out of bed when it's easier to stay there and sleep a bit longer.

Discipline = getting up and getting it done.

Using a coach was (and still is) one of the best investments I've ever made.

Surrounding myself with others to help train and support me, brought an element of structure and accountability to my running.

I believe coaching certainly made a big difference to the time frame it took to achieve my Boston Qualifier time.

Having someone I trusted and believed in, following the training plan they set for me, and knowing I could rely on their wisdom and advice, allowed me build the fitness and mental base I needed.

A good coach can also help you develop your mindset.

In chapter 7, I discussed the mental side of running.

Being strong mentally is similar to building physical strength and resilience.

You have to learn to train your mind. It takes time to make it stronger. Your thoughts create your reality, so be mindful of them. What you tell yourself will have and influence on your actions.

Many times I had to talk to myself, encouraging my body to keep going and push harder, even when I thought I had nothing left in the tank (trust me, you always have a lot more than you think).

There's a saying the goes something like this

'What the mind believes, the body achieves'

And this rings true for me today, as much as it did when I was trying to qualify for Boston.

So by connecting the dots between habit creation, enjoying the process, being consistent, developing discipline, following a plan set by a coach, and working on my mindset, the full picture was starting to take shape.

Now I just needed to sort out the more practical aspects of fuelling (chapter 8),

And work on building physical strength and resilience. Making sure my running form was on point, which I covered in chapter 9.

I would like to say that all went well, and progress was steady and smooth.

However that's not how my story played out, and throughout the journey to get to Boston, I had many setbacks on a physical and personal level.

Probably the biggest test of my mental resilience came when I ran a qualifying marathon under the

Boston qualifying time for my age. I needed 3 hours, 25 minutes, to meet the time standard, and I ran 3 hours, 22 minutes, and 51 seconds.

However, because the entry list was over subscribed, the time for my age category was cut back to 3 hours, 22 minutes, and 32 seconds...

I had missed the new lower qualifying cut off by a mere 19 seconds, basically the time it takes to have a drink of water at an aid station.

I went through every scenario in my head, looking for why I didn't make it. But I realised what it really came down to was one thing. On the day of my qualifying race, my performance wasn't good enough. I had done just enough just to cruise in under what I believed I needed to do.

I knew that I had to work harder, and run a much better qualifying time. So I set to work using what I had learned, and worked on improving on the areas that needed it.

The interesting thing about this, was I discovered I had created a bit of a mental barrier associated with the Boston qualifier time goal.

My training, fitness, and expectations had all been based around running a sub 3:25 marathon, not on running it as fast as I could.

Once I mentally removed this expectation, and focused on running faster with no set time to beat, I knocked 7 mins off my qualifying time in my next race. And then continued to run 2 more subsequent marathons, within a few months of each other, every time getting faster and shaving a total of 11 minutes off my qualifying time.

In life I've found that we are usually given the lesson first, then the opportunity to learn from that lesson.

The pain and disappointment of missing the qualifying time by 19 seconds, pushed me to become better. Without that failure, I probably would have just cruised through the next stage of my running journey. But instead, failure fuelled the fire, and forced me to improve to the point where I would break my mental and physical barriers.

I still apply the same techniques today, I don't settle for mediocrity, I try new things, I make mistakes, and I learn what works, and what doesn't.

So connecting the dots had now revealed the full picture, and I was ready to realise my goal of applying for, and running the Boston marathon.

I first started to work towards qualifying for the Boston Marathon in 2015. I achieved my Boston qualifying marathon in 2016 (3 hours, 18 minutes), and ran my first Boston marathon in 2017 (3hours, 11 mins) .

Chapter 11
What Has Running Taught Me?

At the start of this book I mentioned that this was a collection of stories, and lessons, including the ups-and-downs I encountered in my first few years of running in my mid 40s

It's also a reminder of where I came from, and how hard I worked physically and mentally to make many of the changes I've made over the last several years.

So what does running mean to me? And how has it changed my life?

For me, running, at it's most basic level, brings such a sense of fulfilment. The combination of physical movement, and the way it calms my mind and soul, has helped improve my life in ways I never imagined.

I just feel so much lighter within when I'm running.

It's helped me to grow and manifest change in who I am, and how I act.

It's taught me to be grateful for what I have today, and exposed the best and worst parts of me.

Running is a very honest and simple sport. And like everything in life, its always a work in progress.

I wrote this book as an insight into what worked for me in my formative years as a runner. And I hope you gained some value from what is contained in these pages.

There's so much more to my story, and this book finishes at about the time I left my country of birth (New Zealand), fell in love, and began traveling and exploring the world.

I've visited many different countries, taken part in a variety of races and events, and transformed my lifestyle into one that is very different to the one I had before I began to run.

That's a much bigger story, and one that I can't wait to share with you in my next book.

In closing, I will leave you with you some words of wisdom from one of my coaches, that still rings true today, as much as it did when he first spoke them to me.

'Start from where you are, with what you have, and make the most of every damm day!'

Happy Running everyone

Acknowledgement

Writing this book has been much more challenging than I thought, and at the same time, it's also been an incredibly rewarding experience.

Most importantly, a massive thank you to my wife Fran, who has encouraged and supported me to share my journey. Without her input and feedback on my early drafts, constant support, advice, and the occasional push to keep writing on the days I really lacked the motivation to put pen to paper, (or in todays world, sit in front of a computer screen typing words, when I would rather be outside on the trails).

Thanks for being a positive influence, a kind caring and patient partner. And for encouraging me to share my story with the world.

Secondly, thanks to the people who have

encouraged and helped me with the self publishing process. I really appreciate it.

Also thanks to all the people over the years who have challenged me to become a better version of myself, my past coaches Bevan, who taught me the value of consistency in training. Kerry who introduced me to the wonderful world of ultras, and coached me to some very successful early results.

And my current coach Scotty, who has got me to many start lines in good shape, and always encourages me to do my best, and more importantly, enjoy the journey.

Of course, a big thank you to all my followers and my friends who have been part of this story. This book has happened mostly because of the messages and requests from all of you.

Thanks to my 4 adult kids and my family in New Zealand and Australia, who I miss and love very much.

And lastly, I would like to say how grateful I am for all the setbacks in my life.

The personal struggles, the financial ups-and-downs, the physical health problems, and the mental low points.

They helped me find running at a time in my life when I needed it most.

They taught me valuable lessons that have allowed me to grow into the person I am today.

Running has given me the courage and strength to follow my heart, and pursue my dreams. And I hope it brings as much joy to you, as it has to me...